SLANG

A POCKET GUIDE TO NEW ZEALAND WORDS & PHRASES

So you don't look stupid
when trying to understand
the New Zealand language

PREFACE

New Zealand is home to the Kiwi language but for people from outside the continent, the dialect may sound friendly but foreign.

This mini illustrated 'dictionary' of New Zealand colloquial words, sayings and explanations is here to rescue you.

CHOICE!

ANGUS

Someone with an anger
problem.

*"Bro, that guy is so annoying. I want to
punch him."*
"Bro, don't get all angus."

ARVO

Afternoon.

"Emma is coming round this arvo mate."

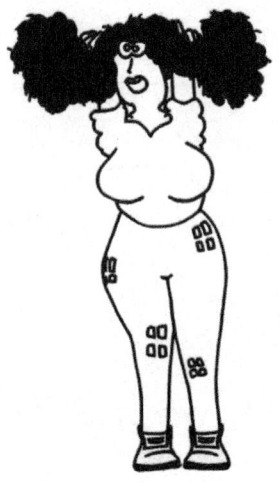

AS

Added to the end of words to place emphasis on the word preceding.

"Emma is loud as!"

BACH

A holiday house usually close to the beach.

"Let's rent out a bach for the weekend."

BEACHED

When you don't want to move
or you're stuck somewhere,
like a whale on a beach.

*"Bro, I don't want to go out. I'm
beached as today."*

BEAUT

Excellent, great.

"That was a beaut little dessert. I feel like a beached whale now."

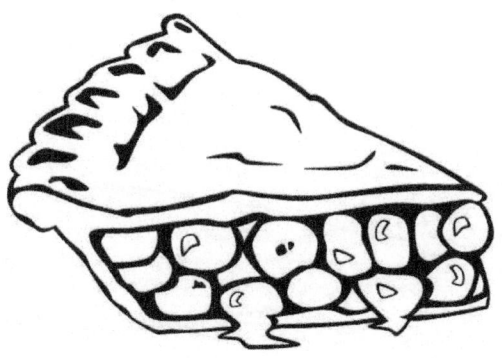

BIG ONE ON THE TURPS

A big night of drinking.

"You can tell he went on a big one on the turps."

BOMB

Something that is cool or awesome.

"This pizza is bomb!"

BOWL ROUND

When someone is coming to visit you.

"I'm going to bowl round your house later."

BRING A PLATE

Bring a shared dish of food to a gathering.

"We asked Emma to bring a plate but she came with an empty one."

#

Used in place of mate, or dude.

"Your attempt at making pancakes looks more like abstract art bro."

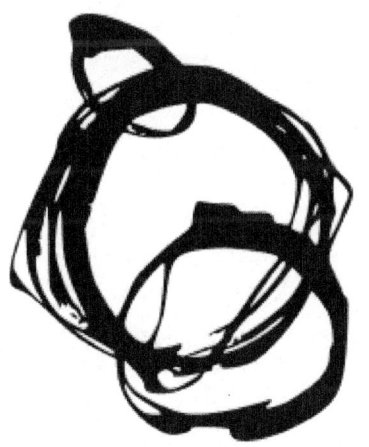

CARK IT

To die.

"Nathan nearly carked it the other day when Emma found out he forgot to wash the dishes."

CHILLY BIN

A cooler.

"The drinks are in the chilly bin."

CHOCKA

Full.

"Emma's wardrobe is chocka and she still goes out shopping."

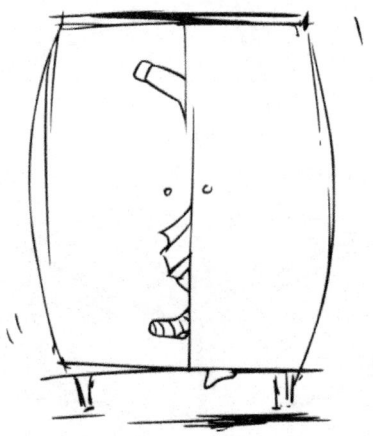

CHOICE

It can be used to mean excellent, awesome, etc.

"We are off to Australia next week."
"That's choice!"

CHOOK

Chicken, used as a term of endearment.

"Hey chook, guess what I have cooked for you tonight."

CHUDDY

Chewing gum.

"Don't swallow your chuddy, it won't digest for 7 years."

CHUR

Used to show gratitude or appreciation. Essentially, a thank you.

"I just found a twenty in my pocket I forgot about. Chur, pants!"

CROOK

Feeling sick or unwell.

"I feel too crook to work today."

CUNT

Often used a term of endearment between friends, but a vulgar term if used as an insult.

"Have you Emma's new boyfriend? He's a good cunt."

CUZ / CUZZY

Like mate or bro, a way to
address a close friend.

"How was your holiday cuz?"

DAG

Funny or quirky person.

"Nathan is a dag when he's in a good mood."

DAIRY

A corner shop or convenience store.

"Get some bread from the dairy."

DRONGO

A fool.

"Don't tell me you forgot to put the beer in the fridge you drongo."

DUNNY

A toilet.

"What are you doing in the dunny?
You've been in there for 45 minutes."

EFTPOS

Electronic Fund Transaction at Point of Sale, the way Kiwis pay for everything. Used to describe both the cash machine and the card swipe in dairies

"I'll pay on Eftpos."

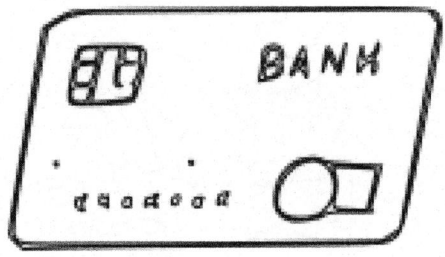

EGG

A clown or a joker.

"You're such an egg."

EH

A word that can be added on to the end of just about any sentence for no reason at all.

"Is this a donkey or an ass, eh?"

FAR OUT

An interjection used to express surprise and awe. It can be used in both a positive and negative light.

"Far out! I just won on this scratchcard."

FULLA

The rest of the world say fella but Kiwis say fulla to refer to a man.

"What a wonderful fulla."

GAP IT

To leave a situation.

"Emma is about to explode, gap it."

GAWK

To stare.

"Look at her gawking at Emma."

GOOD ON YA MATE

Well done.

"Good on ya mate for doing your business outside."

GROTTY

Disgusting.

"Nathan don't be so grotty."

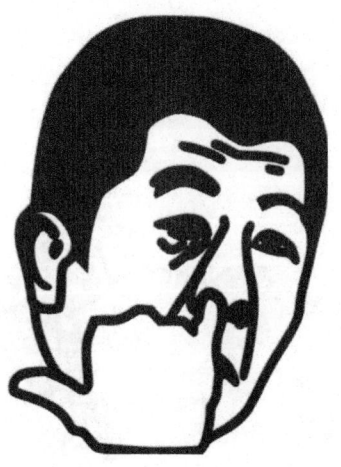

GUMBOOTS

Wellingtons or rubber boots.

"Wear your gum boots, we're going out in the mud today."

HANDLE

A pint of beer.

"Hold my handle for a minute."

HARD OUT

To agree with something.

"New Zealand has the best slang words in the world." Hard out!

HARD YAKKA

Hard work.

"It's hard yakka doing this all day."

HARD-CASE

A person who is funny.

"That Emma makes me laugh, she's a hard case."

HEAPS

A lot.

"I always see that girl heaps."

HOKEY-POKEY

An ice-cream flavour.

"I'll have a large hokey pokey ice-cream please."

HOT CHIPS

Literally, hot chips or french fries.

"I told Emma I'd get her a portion of hot chips but they'll be cold by the time I get home."

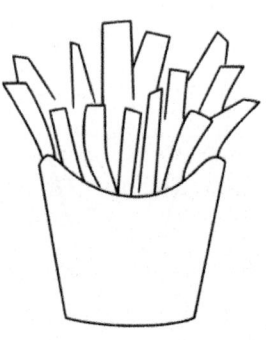

HUNGUS

Someone who eats a lot.

"Leave us some. Don't be a hungus all your life."

JAFA

A fantastic Auklander.

"Oh that looks like a Jafa."

JANDALS

Flip flops.

"My feet just rip right through these jandals."

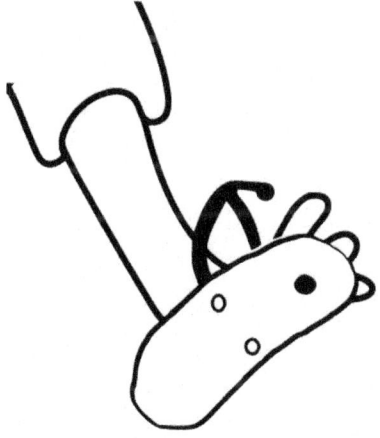

JUDDER BAR

Speed bump.

"I never noticed that judder bar there."

 KIWI

A New Zealander.

"Nathan cannot tell the difference beyween an Aussie and a Kiwi."

LOLLY

A word to describe all sweets,
not just those on a stick.

*"I've got load of lollies from the dairy
for the film tonight."*

LUGGAGE

A major inconvenience.

"Oh that's luggage bro."

MARNUS

When someone is being annoying.

"Stop being marnus Nathan."

MEAN AS

Refers to something being awesome or really good.

"I got a free sandwich." Mean as bro!

MUNTED

When someone is highly intoxicated or something is broken.

"Nathan was munted last night."

NEK MINIT

The next minute. Used when telling a story.

"I was on my bike, nek minit some granny was chasing me."

NOT EVEN

Loosely translates to "No way" or "That's not true."

"Lend me a 20, I'll pay you back." Not even!

OE

Overseas experience after graduating from uni or before they get their first job.

"Nathan is on his OE and looks like he's enjoying the weather in London."

OP SHOP

A charity shop that sells second-hand items. Short for opportunity shop.

"I got this nice dress at the op shop this arvo."

PACK A SAD

To get upset and sulk.

"That kid is packing a sad today."

PAKARU

This Maori word is often used
when something is broken.

"The car is pakaru again."

PANTS

Trousers.

"Nathan you have a stain on your kegs. I'm not washing them for you again."

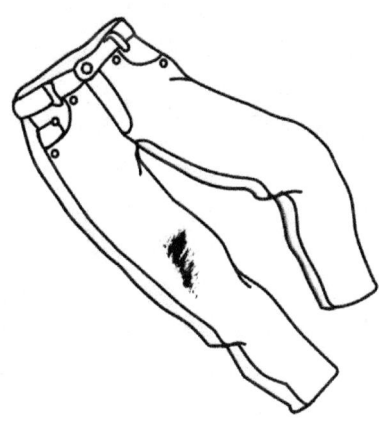

PASH

Kiss.

"Did you hear Nathan and Emma pashed at the party?"

PIKER

Someone who backs out of doing something.

"Mate, stay for the party. Don't be a piker!"

RARK UP

Telling off.

"Emma gave Nathan a good rark up for staying at the party late."

RATTLE
YOUR DAGS

Hurry up.

"Rattle your dags Nathan, we're going to miss the flight."

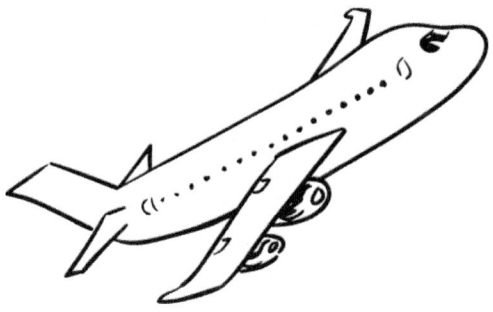

SAMMIE

A sandwich.

"Some people think a jam sammie is weird. But it gets me out of a sticky situation when I don't know what to eat."

SCARFIE

University student

"Nathan thinks he's intelligent ever since he became a scarfie."

SCROGGIN

Trail mix, an ideal source of energy when on an outdoor adventure.

"Stop picking all the good stuff out of the scroggin!"

SCULL

To down a drink in one go.

"Happy birthday. Now scull that beer!"

SHARN

A conversation but not really
having a decent one.

*"I don't like Emma but I just had a
sharn with her to be friendly."*

SHE'LL BE RIGHT

Everything will be okay.

"Are the sausages burning?"
"Nah, she'll be alright."

SKUX

A versatile expression with the most popular meaning is when someone looks cool or trendy. It can also be used for when a person is looking hot.

"You look skux today."

SMOKO

A cigarette break.

"He's gone for another smoko."

SNAG

Sausage.

"Throw a few snags on the barbie for me."

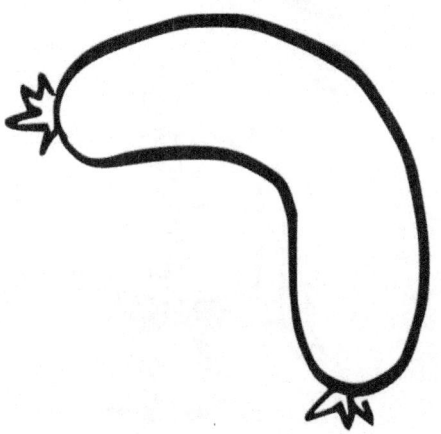

SPINNING YARNS

Having a conversation with some exaggeration involved.

"She was spinning yarns after she had a few drinks."

SQUIZ

To have a look at something.

"This is what happened when Nathan first had a squiz at Emma."

STINK ONE

An expression used when you're a little disappointed.

"I don't have any money to lend you."
"Oh stink one bro."

STOKED

Very happy about something.

"I was stoked to see my favourite animal."

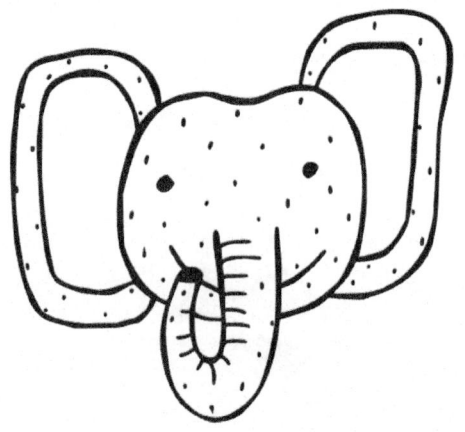

STUBBIE

A bottle of beer.

"Have a stubbie before you die of thirst."

STUBBIES

A pair of very short shorts.

"Get your stubbies on, we're going to the beach."

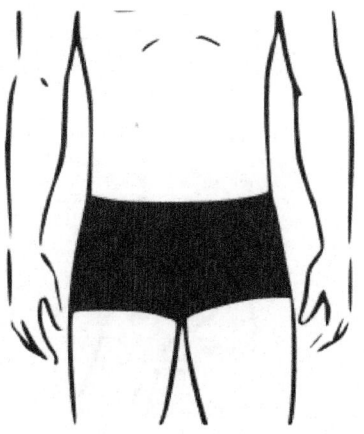

SWEET AS

A way of saying "thank you", "no worries", "you're welcome", "it's all good" or "that's cool".

"This tune is sweet as."

TIKI TOUR

To go the long way to a
destination or just a long drive
with no purpose.

*"Let's head out for a tiki tour in your
new car."*

TOGS

Swimwear.

"I'm in the pool with my togs on"

TRAMPING

Hiking.

"Nathan and Emma have gone out tramping."

TU MEKE

The Māori translation is 'too much'. A way of expressing gratitude for generous acts, a way of saying thank you.

"I got you some milk."
"Too much!"

TURPS

Alcohol.

"Emma's been on the turps again."

UNDIES

Underwear.

"Nathan you need to buy some new undies."

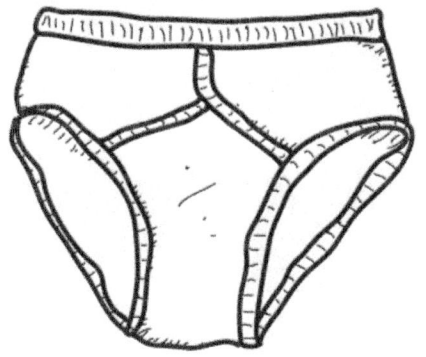

WESTIE

Someone from West Auckland.

"Emma is a Westie."

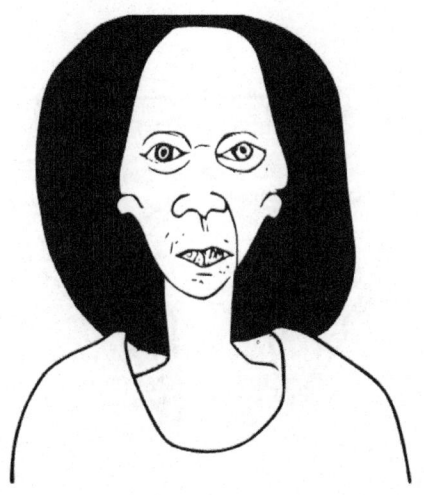

WOP WOPS

The middle of nowhere.

"They live out in the wop wops."

YARN

To have a chat or tell a story.

"That was a good yarn."

YEAH, NAH

A phrase than can mean yes, no or maybe but generally The New Zealand way of saying no.

"You looked really ill on Friday." Yeah-nah I was fine.

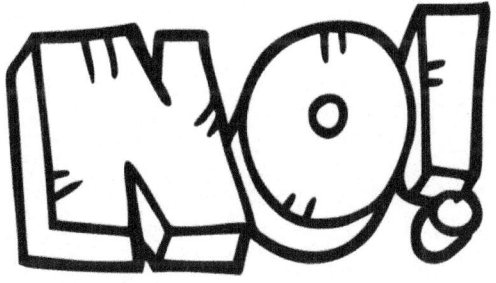

A

A&P SHOW
Agricultural & Pastoral Show.

ADS
TV commercials, advertisements.

ALL BLACKS
New Zealand Rugby Team.

ALL WHITES
New Zealand Soccer Team.

ANGUS
Someone with an anger problem.

ANKLEBITER
Toddler, small child.

ANZAC
Australian and New Zealand Army Corps.

AOTEAROA
Maori name for New Zealand meaning land of the long white cloud.

AROHA
Maori word for love.

ARVO
Afternoon.

AS
Added to the end of words to place emphasis on the word preceding.

B

BABY BLACKS
New Zealand Junior Rugby Team.

BACH
Holiday house (North Island term, derived from 'bachelor home').

BANGER
A sausage or old car.

BARBIE
Barbecue.

BEACHED
When you're stuck somewhere, like a whale on a beach.

BEAUT
Excellent, great.

BIG SMOKE
Large town or city.

BIKKIE
A biscuit.

BIT OF A PROBLEM
A real worry.

BIT OF DAG
Hard case, comedian, person with character.

BITSER
Mongrel dog.

BLACK CAPS
New Zealand Cricket Team.

BLACK STICKS
New Zealand Hockey Team.

BLOKE
A man.

BLOW ME DOWN!
What a surprise, I didn't know that.

BLUDGER
Somebody who tries to get something for free.

BOBBY CALF
Young male calf.

BOMB
Something that is cool or awesome.

BOWL ROUND
When someone is coming to visit you.

BOY RACER
Is a term New Zealander's use when they are referring to youth or young men driving fast cars that they have generally modified.

BRASSED OFF
Annoyed.

BREKKIE
Breakfast.

BRICKIE
Bricklayer.

BRING A PLATE
Bring a plate of food to a dinner or a party.

BRO
Used in place of mate, or dude..

BROLLY
Umbrella.

BROWN EYE
To flash your naked butt at someone.

BUGGER
Damn!.

BUGGER ALL
Not much, hardly anything.

BUNGY
Kiwi slang for elastic strap, as in Bungy
Jumping.

BUSH
Native forest.

BUSHED
Exhausted.

BUST YOUR GUTS
Make a huge effort.

BUZZY BEE
Iconic New Zealand wooden toy.

BYO
Bring Your Own (alcohol into a restaurant for example).

CARAVAN
Mobile home that you tow behind your car.

CARDI
Cardigan.

CARK IT
To die.

CARKED
Fallen over or died.

CAST
Immobilised, unable to get to your feet.

CHEERIO
Goodbye.

CHEERIO
Name for a cocktail sausage.

CHEERS
Thanks.

CHICK
Slang word for woman/female.

CHILLY BIN
Cool box for a picnic to store cold items.

CHINWAG
Conversation.

CHIPPIE
A carpenter.

CHIPS
French Fries.

CHOCKA
Full, overflowing.

CHOICE!
Great!

CHOOK
Chicken.

CHRISSY PRESSIES
Christmas presents.

CHUDDY
Chewing gum.

CHUFFED
Proud and happy.

CHUNDER
Vomit, throw up.

CHUR
A parting remark like cheers as in 'Chur bro.'

COASTER
A resident or ex-resident of the west coast of the South Island.

COCKIE
Farmer.

COTTON BUDS
Q-tips.

CREEK
Small stream.

CRIB
Holiday house (South Island term).

CROOK
Feeling sick or unwell.

CUNT
Often used a term of endearment between friends, but a vulgar term if used as an insult.

CUPPA
Cup of tea or coffee.

CUZ / CUZZY
Like mate or bro, a way to address a close friend.

D

DAG
A bit of a joker. Dags can also be found on a sheep's bottom.

DAIRY
A corner shop or convenience store.

DE FACTO
Name used for a couple who are not married but are living together.

DING
Small dent in a vehicle.

DODGY
Bad, unreliable, not good.

DOING A DONUT
Boyracers spinning their cars in a tight circle.

DOLE
Unemployment benefit.

DOWN THE GURGLER
Failed plan.

DRONGO
Stupid fool, idiot.

DROP YOUR GEAR
Take your clothes off, get undressed.

DUNGER
A run down property.

DUNNY
Toilet, bathroom, lavatory.

DUVET
Quilt, doona.

E

EAR BASHING
Someone talking incessantly.

EASY AS
No problem.

EFTPOS
Electronic Fund Transaction at Point of Sale,
the way Kiwis pay for everything. Used to
describe both the cash machine and the card
swipe in dairies.

EGG
A clown or a joker.

EH
A word that can be added on to the end of just about any sentence for no reason at all.

ENTREE
Appetizer, hors d'oeurve.

F

FAR OUT
An interjection used to express surprise and awe. .

FEED
Meal.

FIZZ BOAT
Small power boat.

FIZZY DRINK
Soda pop.

FLANNEL
Wash cloth, face cloth.

FLAT
Apartment, name for rental accommodation
that is shared.

FLAT OUT
A term New Zealander's use when they are very
busy.

FLICKS
Movies, picture theatre.

FLOG
Steal, rob.

FOOTIE
Rugby union or league (not soccer).

FOOTROT FLATS
Famous comic books about typical Kiwi rural life.

FOOTY
Rugby.

FULL TILT
Going very fast, using all your power.

FULLA
The rest of the world say fella but Kiwis say fulla to refer to a man.

G

G'DAY
Universal Kiwi greeting, also spelled gidday.

G'DAY GUYS
A greeting you say to people you don't really
know as you walk pass, applies to any gender
even pets.

GAP IT
To leave a situation.

GAWK
To stare.

GET OFF THE GRASS
Get real.

GET THE WILLIES
Overcome with trepidation.

GODZONE
God's own country, New Zealand.

GOING BUSH
Take a break, become reclusive.

GOOD AS GOLD
Feeling good, not a problem, yes.

GOOD ON YA MATE
Well done.

GOOD ON YA, MATE!
Congratulations, well done, proud of someone.

GOOD SORT
A good person.

GREASIES
Fish and chips.

GROTTY
Disgusting.

GUMBOOTS
Rubber boots or Wellies, originally gumdigger boots.

GUMDIGGER
Finding buried Kauri gum (hardened resin).

GUMMIES
Rubber boots, wellingtons. Gumboots.

GUTTED
Disappointed.

H

HANDLE
Pint of beer.

HAPPY AS LARRY
Very happy.

HARD CASE
Amusing, funny person.

HARD OUT
To agree with something.

HARD YAKKA
Hard work.

HARD-CASE
A person who is funny.

HAVE A GO
Try something.

HEAPS
A lot.

HIGHTAIL
Retreat as fast as possible.

HISSY FIT
A tantrum.

HOKEY POKEY
Icecream with vanilla flavour and honey comb bits.

HOKEY-POKEY
An ice-cream flavour.

HOLLYWOOD
To fake or exaggerate an injury on the sportsfield.

HOME AND HOSED
Safe, successfully finished, completed.

HOON
A young fast driver in a car.

HOSING DOWN
Heavy rain, raining heavily.

HOT CHIPS
Literally, hot chips or french fries.

HOTTIE
Hot water bottle or attractive person.

HOW'S IT GOING MATE?
Kiwi greeting.

HUI
Meeting.

HUNGUS
Someone who eats a lot.

HUNTAWAY
Dog bred for barking skills.

I

ICEBLOCK
Popsicle, Ice Stick.

IN THE STICKS
Rural.

IN YONKS, IN DONKEY'S YEARS
For a very long time.

J

JAFA
An Aucklander.

JAFFA
Chocolate orange bikkie and type of seedless
Orange.

JANDALS
Japanese sandals - Known as flip flops to some
and thongs to others.

JOKER
A regular bloke.

JUDDER BAR
Speed bump.

JUG
A water kettle or large measure of beer.

JUMPER
Sweater, jersey.

K

KAI
'Food' in Maori language.

KIA ORA
Maori word for hi.

KICK THE BUCKET
Die.

KIWI
A flightless bird.

KIWI
New Zealander.

KIWI FRUIT
Brown furry skinned fruit, Zespri, Chinese Gooseberry.

KNACKERED
Exhausted, tired, lethargic.

KNUCKLE SANDWHICH
A fist in the teeth, punch in the mouth.

KOHA
Gift.

KUMARA
Sweet potato.

L

L&P
Lemon & Paeroa - a drink 'World famous in New Zealand.'

LAUGHING GEAR
Mouth, as in wrap your laughing gear around this.

LIFT
Elevator.

LIKE A BOX OF BUDGIES
Very happy.

LOLLY
Any kind of sweet confectionary.

LONGDROP
Outside composting toilet.

LOO
Bathroom, toilet.

LUCKED IN
In luck.

LUGGAGE
A major inconvenience.

LURGY
Flu.

M

MACCAS
The fast food establishment, McDonald's.

MAD AS A MEAT AXE
Very angry or crazy.

MAIN
Primary dish of a meal.

MAINLAND
The South Island.

MAORI
Indigenous New Zealander.

MARAE
Maori meeting house.

MARNUS
When someone is being annoying.

MATE
A friend.

MEAN AS
Refers to something being awesome or really good.

METAL ROAD
Unsealed gravel road.

MOTORWAY
Freeway.

MOUNTAIN OYSTERS
Ram testicles.

MUCKING IN
Helping.

MUNTED
When someone is highly intoxicated or something is broken.

MUNTED
When something is broken or damaged.

N

NAFF OFF
Go away, get lost, leave me alone.

NAH YEAH
The New Zealand way of saying yes.

NANA
Grandmother, grandma.

NAPPY
Diaper.

NEK MINIT
The next minute. Used when telling a story.

NEK MINNIT
A phrased used when something happens next minute.

NO WORRIES
No problem.

NORTH CAPE TO THE BLUFF
From one end of New Zealand to the other.

NOT EVEN
Loosely translates to "No way" or "That's not true."

NUMBER 8 WIRE
Is a term used for the ingenuity and resourcefulness of New Zealanders.

OE
Overseas Experience, many students go on their OE after finishing university, see the world.

OFFSIDER
An assistant, someones friend.

OLD BOMB
Old car.

OLDIES
Parents.

ON THE NEVER NEVER
Paying for something using layby, not paying straight away.

ON THE TURPS
When someone has had a big night out drinking alcohol.

OP SHOP
A charity shop that sells second-hand items. Short for opportunity shop.

OPEN SLATHER
A free-for-all.

OVER THE DITCH
The ditch is favourably known as the Tasman
Sea that separates New Zealand and Australia.

P

PACK A SAD
Bad mood, morose, ill-humoured, broken.

PADDOCK
Field, be it for grazing or sports.

PAKARU
This Maori word is often used when something
is broken.

PAKEHA
New Zealander of European origin or non-
Maori person.

PANEL BEATER
Auto repair shop, panel shop.

PANTS
Trousers.

PASH
Kiss.

PAV
Pavlova, dessert usually topped with kiwifruit and cream.

PAVLOVA
New Zealand dessert with fruit, cream and meringue.

PERVE
To stare.

PETROL
Gasoline, gas.

PIECE-OF-PISS
Easy, not hard to do.

PIKE OUT
Chicken out of something.

PIKELET
Small pancake usually had with jam and
whipped cream.

PIKER
Someone who backs out of doing something.

PIKER
Someone who gives up easy, slacker.

PINKY
Little finger.

PISS AROUND
Waste time, muck around.

PISS UP
Party, social gathering, excuse for drinking alcohol.

PISSED OFF
Annoyed, angry, upset.

PISSHEAD
Someone who drinks a lot of alcohol, heavy drinker.

PLONK
Is a term New Zealander's use for a cheap bottle of wine.

POKIES
A gambling machine.

POM
'Prisoner of Mother England' - half-derogatory for an English person.

PONG
Bad smell, stink.

POSTAL CODE
Zip code.

PRAM
Baby stroller, baby pushchair.

PRANG
A crash, vehicle accident.

PRESSIE
Present.

PUB
Bar or hotel that serves alcohol.

PUDDING
Dessert.

PUSHING UP DAISIES
Dead and buried.

Q

QUACK
Medical doctor.

R

RANDY
Horny, wanting sex.

RARK UP
Telling somebody off.

RATBAG
Unpleasant or malicious person, but used fondly in the case of mischievous children.

RATTLE YOUR DAGS
Hurry up, get moving.

RELLIES
Relatives, family.

RESERVE
Public recreational area.

RING
To telephone somebody, as in "I'll give you a ring."

ROOT
Have sex, get sex.

ROPEABLE
Very angry.

RSA
The Royal New Zealand Returned and Services' Association.

RUBBISH
Garbage, trash.

RUST BUCKET
Decrepit motor car.

S

SAMMIE
A sandwich.

SAV
A saveloy (sausage).

SCARCE AS HENS TEETH
Very rare.

SCARFIE
University student.

SCROGGIN
Trampers high energy food including dried fruits, chocolate.

SCULL
Consume, drink quickly.

SERVIETTE
Paper napkin.

SHANDY
Drink made with lemonade and beer.

SHARK AND TATIES
Fish and chips.

SHARN
A conversation but not really having a decent one.

SHEILA
A woman/female.

SHE'LL BE RIGHT
All will be ok.

SHIT A BRICK
Exclamation of surprise or annoyance.

SHOOT THROUGH
To leave suddenly.

SHOUT
To treat, to buy something for someone.

SICKIE
To take a day off work or school because you are sick.

SILVER FERNS
New Zealand Netball Team.

SKITE
To boast, boasting, bragging.

SKODY
Gross, disgusting.

SKUX
When someone looks cool or trendy. It can also be used for when a person is looking hot.

SMOKO
Once 'Smoking break', now commonly used for taking a work break.

SNAG
Sausage.

SNARLER
Sausage.

SNOWED UNDER
Used to indicate you are very busy and have too much work to do.

SOOK
Cry baby, wimp.

SPARKIE
Electrician.

SPARROW FART
Very early in the morning, sunrise.

SPIN A YARN
When someone embellishes a story that is often long and drawn out and it generally isn't factual.

SPINNING YARNS
Having a conversation with some exaggeration involved.

SPROG
Child.

SPUD
Potato.

SQUIZ
Take a quick look.

STAGGY
Stagnant.

STATION
Large farm.

STEINIE
Bottle of Steinlager, brand lager.

STINK ONE
An expression used when you're a little disappointed.

STOKED
Used for when they are happy about something.

STRAPPED FOR CASH
Low on cash, no money.

STUBBIE
Small bottle of beer.

STUBBIES
Very short men's shorts.

STUBBY
Small glass bottle of beer.

SUNDAY DRIVER
Someone who drives very slow.

SUNNIES
Sunglasses.

SUS
Suspicious.

SWANNDRI
Typical outdoor clothing for farmers.

SWEET
A way of saying "thank you", "no worries", "you're welcome", "it's all good" or "that's cool".

SWEET AS
Great!

T

TA
Thanks.

TAKE-AWAYS
Food to be taken away and eaten, fast food outlet.

TALL BLACKS
New Zealand Basketball Team.

TEA
A cuppa or evening meal.

THE OLDS
One's parents.

TIGHTS
Pantyhose.

TIKI TOUR
Is what Kiwis say when they take a scenic route to a destination or a scenic tour of an area.

TINNY
Small metal boat.

TOGS
Swimsuit, bathing costume.

TORCH
Flashlight.

TOWNIES
City people.

TRAMP STAMP
A tattoo on a woman's lower back.

TRAMPING
Hiking.

TRUE
Really?.

TU MEKE
The Maori translation is 'too much'. A way of expressing gratitude for generous acts.

TURPS
Alcohol.

TWINK
White-out.

U

UNDIES
Underwear.

UNI
University.

UP THE DUFF
Pregnant.

UTE
Utility vehicle or pickup truck.

V

VARSITY
University.

VEGES
Vegetables.

W

WALLY
Clown, silly person.

WE'LL SEE YOU RIGHT
Don't worry we'll make sure you're ok.

WELLYWOOD
The nickname for New Zealand's film industry centred on Wellington.

WESTIE
Someone from West Aukland.

WHANAU
Extended family.

WHINGE
Complain, moan.

WOBBLY
To have a tantrum.

WOP-WOPS
Situated off the beaten track, out of the way location.

Y

YACK
To have a conversation with a friend, to talk.

YARN
To have a chat or tell a story.

YEAH NAH
Is what New Zealander's say with indecision. It's a phrase than can mean yes, no or maybe.

YONKS
A very long time.

YOUSE

'You' plural.

GAP IT

GAP IT

GAP IT

GAP IT

GAP IT

GAP IT

GAP IT

GAP IT

GAP IT

Printed in Great Britain
by Amazon

57226115R00086